The Armband B

Written by Hazel Townson
Illustrated by Scoular Anderson

Collins Educational
An imprint of HarperCollinsPublishers

Last term, orange armbands were the latest craze.

It all started when Sam Archer's
mum made him wear one to school.

Sam hated the thing.
He said it made him feel like a real wimp.

So he gave it to Rachel Clark who sat behind him.

Orange was Rachel's favourite colour.
The armband looked good with her yellow
anorak as well as her blonde hair.

At break-time Rachel marched round the playground with the armband on, chanting:
"I'm in the Armband Band!"
The idea caught on…

Next day, there were two girls and two boys wearing orange armbands. They all marched round, chanting: "We're in the Armband Band!"

So then Sam Archer wanted his armband back.
He said *he* started the Armband Band, it was his idea,
and Rachel Clark could go and buy her own.

Next day, Rachel turned up with two orange armbands, one for each arm, and said that was the only way to be a proper member of the Armband Band.

Sam Archer was only half a member, if that!

So then *everybody* got two armbands, and soon nearly the whole school was marching round the playground, chanting: "We're in the Armband Band!"

Mr Pickles, who sold the armbands at the corner shop, couldn't believe his luck!

Next day, *nobody* wore an orange armband.
But Sam Archer turned up with a set of stickers that glowed in the dark...